John Wilbur Chapman

Received ye the Holy Ghost?

John Wilbur Chapman

Received ye the Holy Ghost?

ISBN/EAN: 9783337284121

Printed in Europe, USA, Canada, Australia, Japan

Cover: Foto ©Lupo / pixelio.de

More available books at **www.hansebooks.com**

Received Ye The Holy Ghost?

By J. WILBUR CHAPMAN, D.D.

AUTHOR OF
"THE IVORY PALACES OF THE KING," ETC.

FLEMING H. REVELL COMPANY
NEW YORK
CHICAGO
TORONTO

PUBLISHERS
OF EVANGELICAL
LITERATURE

TO

Mr. D. L. Moody

AND TO

Rev. F. B. Meyer

THIS BOOK IS GRATEFULLY DEDICATED

To the former, because in his public ministry and private life he has been a great inspiration. To the latter, because two years ago, in a single sentence, he opened up a new life to me when he led me to know more about the Spirit of God.

Under God, to both of these, his servants, I owe an inexpressible debt of gratitude.

CONTENTS

CAP	PAGE
1. What saith the Scripture?...........	9
2. How may I Know Him?..................	31
3. How may I Receive Him?..............	65
4. What of the Result?..................	101

RECEIVED YE THE HOLY GHOST?

WHAT SAITH THE SCRIPTURE?

Cap I
WHAT SAITH THE SCRIPTURE?

"Search the Scriptures; for in them ye think ye have eternal life: and they are they which testify of me."—John v. 39.

ATTRIBUTES OF THE HOLY SPIRIT.—Gen. i. 2: And the Spirit of God moved upon the face of the waters. Job xxxiii. 4: The Spirit of God hath made me, and the breath of the Almighty hath given me life. Ps. cxxxix. 7: Whither shall I go from thy Spirit? or whither shall I flee from thy presence? Isa. xl. 13: Who hath directed the Spirit of the Lord, or being his counselor hath taught him? Zech. iv. 6: Not by might, nor by power, but by my Spirit, saith the Lord of hosts. Luke i. 35: The Holy Ghost shall come upon thee, and the power of the Highest shall overshadow thee: therefore also that holy thing which shall be born of thee shall be called the Son of God. John vi. 63: It is the Spirit that quickeneth. Acts v. 3: Why hath Satan filled thine heart to lie to the Holy Ghost? 4: Thou hast not lied unto men, but unto God. 1 Cor. ii. 10: But God hath revealed them unto us by his Spirit: for the Spirit searcheth all things, yea, the deep things of God. 11: For what man knoweth the things of a man, save the spirit of man which is in him? even so the things of God knoweth no man, but the Spirit of God. Heb. ix. 14: The eternal Spirit. Heb. x. 29: The Spirit of grace. 1 Peter iv. 14: The Spirit of glory and of God resteth upon you. Rev. iv. 5: Seven lamps of fire burning before the throne, which are the seven Spirits of God. Rev. xi. 11: The Spirit of life from God.

MIRACULOUS INFLUENCES OF THE HOLY SPIRIT.—Joel ii. 28, 29: And it shall come to pass afterward, that I will pour out my Spirit upon all flesh; and your sons and your daughters shall prophesy, your old men shall dream dreams, your young men shall see visions: and also upon the servants and upon the handmaids in those days will I pour out my Spirit. Matt. xii. 28: But if I cast out devils by the Spirit of God, then the kingdom of

God is come unto you. Acts i. 5, 8: For John truly baptized with water; but ye shall be baptized with the Holy Ghost not many days hence. But ye shall receive power, after that the Holy Ghost is come upon you: and ye shall be witnesses unto me both in Jerusalem, and in all Judea, and in Samaria, and unto the uttermost part of the earth. Acts ii. 2–4: And suddenly there came a sound from heaven as of a rushing mighty wind, and it filled all the house where they were sitting. And there appeared unto them cloven tongues like as of fire, and it sat upon each of them. And they were all filled with the Holy Ghost, and began to speak with other tongues, as the Spirit gave them utterance. Acts viii. 15–17: Who, when they were come down, prayed for them, that they might receive the Holy Ghost: (for as yet he was fallen upon none of them: only they were baptized in the name of the Lord Jesus.) Then laid they their hands on them, and they received the Holy Ghost. Acts x. 44, 46: While Peter yet spake these words, the Holy Ghost fell on all them which heard the word. For they heard them speak with tongues, and magnify God. Acts xix. 2–6: He said unto them, Have ye received the Holy Ghost since ye believed? And they said unto him, We have not so much as heard whether there be any Holy Ghost. And he said unto them, Unto what then were ye baptized? And they said, Unto John's baptism. Then said Paul, John verily baptized with the baptism of repentance, saying unto the people, that they should believe on him which should come after him, that is, on Christ Jesus. When they heard this, they were baptized in the name of the Lord Jesus. And when Paul had laid his hands upon them, the Holy Ghost came on them; and they spake with tongues, and prophesied. 1 Cor. xii. 9–11: To another faith by the same Spirit; to another the gifts of healing by the same Spirit; to another the working of miracles; to another prophecy; to another discerning of spirits; to another divers kinds of tongues; to another the interpretation of tongues: but all these worketh that one and the selfsame Spirit, dividing to every man severally as he will. Gal. iii. 5: He therefore that ministereth to you the Spirit, and worketh miracles among you, doeth he it by the works of the law, or by the hearing of faith? Heb. ii. 4: God also bearing them witness, both with signs and wonders, and with divers miracles, and gifts of the Holy Ghost, according to his own will.

PRAYER FOR THE HOLY SPIRIT.—Ps. li. 11: Take not thy Holy Spirit from me. 12: Uphold me with thy free Spirit. Luke xi. 13: If ye then, being evil, know how to give good gifts unto your children: how much more shall your heavenly Father give the Holy Spirit to them that ask him? Acts iv. 31: When they had prayed, the place was shaken where they were assembled together; and they were all filled with the Holy Ghost. Eph. iii. 16: That he would grant you, according to the riches of his glory, to be strengthened with might by his Spirit in the inner man.

SINS AGAINST THE HOLY SPIRIT.—
Isa. lxiii. 10: They rebelled, and vexed his Holy Spirit: therefore he was turned to be their enemy. Matt. xii. 31: But the blasphemy against the Holy Ghost shall not be forgiven unto men. 32: And whosoever speaketh a word against the Son of man, it shall be forgiven him: but whosoever speaketh against the Holy Ghost, it shall not be forgiven him, neither in this world, neither in the world to come. Mark iii. 29: But he that shall blaspheme against the Holy Ghost hath never forgiveness, but is in danger of eternal damnation. Acts vii. 51: Ye do always resist the Holy Ghost: as your fathers did, so do ye. Acts viii. 18–20: And when Simon saw that through laying on of the Apostles' hands the Holy Ghost was

given, he offered them money, saying, Give me also this power, that on whomsoever I lay hands, he may receive the Holy Ghost. But Peter said unto him, Thy money perish with thee, because thou hast thought that the gift of God may be purchased with money. Eph. iv. 30: Grieve not the Holy Spirit of God. 1 Thess. v. 19: Quench not the Spirit. Heb. x. 29: Of how much sorer punishment, suppose ye, shall he be thought worthy, who hath . . . done despite unto the Spirit of grace? Rev. ii. 7: He that hath an ear, let him hear what the Spirit saith unto the churches.

THE WORK AND INFLUENCE OF THE HOLY SPIRIT.—Gen. vi. 3: My Spirit shall not always strive with man. Isa. xliv. 3: For I will pour water upon him that is thirsty, and floods upon the dry ground: I will pour my Spirit upon thy seed, and my blessing upon thine offspring. 4: And they shall spring up as among the grass, as willows by the watercourses. Isa. lix. 19: When the enemy shall come in like a flood, the Spirit of the Lord shall lift up a standard against him. 21: My Spirit that is upon thee, and my words which I have put in thy mouth, shall not depart out of thy mouth, nor out of the mouth of thy seed. Ezek. xxxix. 29: Neither will I hide my face any more from them: for I have poured out my Spirit upon the house of Israel. Hag. ii. 5: According to the word that I covenanted with you when ye came out of Egypt, so my Spirit remaineth among you. Zech. xii. 10: I will pour upon the house of David, and upon the inhabitants of Jerusalem, the spirit of grace and of supplications: and they shall look upon me whom they have pierced, and they shall mourn. Matt. iii. 11: I indeed baptize you with water unto repentance: but . . . he shall baptize you with the Holy Ghost, and with fire. John iv. 14: Whosoever drinketh of the water that I shall give him shall never thirst; but the water that I shall give him shall be in him a well of water springing up into everlasting life. John vii. 38: He that believeth on me, as the Scripture hath said, out of his belly shall flow rivers of living water. 39: (But this spake he of the Spirit, which they that believe on him should receive: for the Holy Ghost was not yet given; because that Jesus was not yet glorified.) John xiv. 16, 17: I will pray the

Father, and he shall give you another Comforter, that he may abide with you forever; even the Spirit of truth; whom the world cannot receive, because it seeth him not, neither knoweth him: but ye know him; for he dwelleth with you, and shall be in you. John xv. 26: When the Comforter is come, whom I will send unto you from the Father, even the Spirit of truth, which proceedeth from the Father, he shall testify of me. John xvi. 7: It is expedient for you that I go away: for if I go not away, the Comforter will not come unto you; but if I depart, I will send him unto you. 8: When he is come, he will reprove the world of sin, and of righteousness, and of judgment. John xx. 22: He breathed on them, and saith unto them, Receive ye the Holy Ghost. Acts

ii. 38: Repent, and be baptized every one of you in the name of Jesus Christ for the remission of sins, and ye shall receive the gift of the Holy Ghost. Acts iii. 19: That your sins may be blotted out, when the times of refreshing shall come from the presence of the Lord. Acts v. 32: We are his witnesses of these things; and so is also the Holy Ghost, whom God hath given to them that obey him. Acts vi. 5: They chose Stephen, a man full of faith and of the Holy Ghost. Acts ix. 31: Walking in the fear of the Lord, and in the comfort of the Holy Ghost, were multiplied. Acts x. 44: The Holy Ghost fell on all them which heard the word. 45: And they of the circumcision which believed were astonished, as many as came with Peter, because that on the Gentiles also was poured out the gift of the Holy Ghost. Acts xi. 24: He was a good man, and full of the Holy Ghost. Acts xiii. 52: The disciples were filled with joy, and with the Holy Ghost. Acts xv. 8: God, which knoweth the hearts, bare them witness, giving them the Holy Ghost, even as he did unto us. Rom. viii. 11: If the Spirit of him that raised up Jesus from the dead dwell in you, he that raised up Christ from the dead shall also quicken your mortal bodies by his Spirit that dwelleth in you. 14: As many as are led by the Spirit of God, they are the sons of God. 23: Not only they, but ourselves also, which have the first-fruits of the Spirit. Rom. viii. 26: The Spirit also helpeth our infirmities: for we know not what we should pray for as we ought: but the

Spirit itself maketh intercession for us with groanings which cannot be uttered. 27: And he that searcheth the hearts knoweth what is the mind of the Spirit, because he maketh intercession for the saints according to the will of God. Rom. xv. 13: That ye may abound in hope, through the power of the Holy Ghost. 1 Cor. ii. 4: Not with enticing words of man's wisdom, but in demonstration of the Spirit and of power. 1 Cor. iii. 16: Know ye not that ye are the temple of God, and that the Spirit of God dwelleth in you? 1 Cor. xii. 4: Now there are diversities of gifts, but the same Spirit. 7: The manifestation of the Spirit is given to every man to profit withal. 9: To another faith by the same Spirit. 2 Cor. i. 22: Who hath also sealed us, and given the earnest of the

Spirit in our hearts. Gal. iv. 6: Because ye are sons, God hath sent forth the Spirit of his Son into your hearts, crying, Abba, Father. Gal. v. 5: We through the Spirit wait for the hope of righteousness by faith. 16: Walk in the Spirit, and ye shall not fulfil the lust of the flesh. 17: For the flesh lusteth against the Spirit, and the Spirit against the flesh: and these are contrary the one to the other; so that ye cannot do the things that ye would. 18: But if ye be led of the Spirit, ye are not under the law. 25: If we live in the Spirit, let us also walk in the Spirit. Gal. vi. 8: He that soweth to the Spirit shall of the Spirit reap life everlasting. Eph. i. 13, 14: After that ye believed, ye were sealed with that Holy Spirit of promise, which is the earnest of our inheritance until the redemption of the purchased possession, unto the praise of his glory. Eph. ii. 18: Through him we both have access by one Spirit unto the Father. 22: In whom ye also are builded together for a habitation of God through the Spirit. Eph. iv. 3: Endeavoring to keep the unity of the Spirit in the bond of peace. 4: There is one body, and one Spirit, even as ye are called in one hope of your calling. 30: The Holy Spirit of God, whereby ye are sealed unto the day of redemption. Eph. v. 9: The fruit of the Spirit is in all goodness and righteousness and truth. 18: Be filled with the Spirit. Eph. vi. 18: Praying always with all prayer and supplication in the Spirit. Phil. i. 19: This shall turn to my salvation through your prayer, and the supply of the Spirit

RECEIVED YE THE HOLY GHOST?

of Jesus Christ. 1 Thess. i. 5: Our gospel came not unto you in word only, but also in power, and in the Holy Ghost. 6: Having received the word in much affliction, with joy of the Holy Ghost. 2 Tim. i. 7: God hath not given us the spirit of fear; but of power, and of love, and of a sound mind. 14: That good thing which was committed unto thee keep by the Holy Ghost which dwelleth in us. 1 John iii. 24: We know that he abideth in us, by the Spirit which he hath given us. 1 John iv. 2: Hereby know ye the Spirit of God: Every spirit that confesseth that Jesus Christ is come in the flesh is of God. 13: Hereby know we that we dwell in him, and he in us, because he hath given us of his Spirit. 1 John v. 6: It is the Spirit that beareth witness, because the Spirit is truth.

7: For there are three that bear record in heaven, the Father, the Word, and the Holy Ghost: and these three are one. 8: And there are three that bear witness in earth, the spirit, and the water, and the blood: and these three agree in one. Jude 20: Building up yourselves on your most holy faith, praying in the Holy Ghost. Rev. i. 4: Grace be unto you, and peace, from . . . the seven Spirits which are before his throne. Rev. xxii. 17: The Spirit and the bride say, Come.

RECEIVED
YE THE
HOLY GHOST?

HOW MAY
I KNOW HIM?

Cap II   *HOW MAY I KNOW HIM?*

"Afterward he brought me again unto the door of the house; and, behold, waters issued out from under the threshold of the house eastward."—Ezek. xlvii. 1.

NOTHING could be more important, in these days, than a clear discernment of the character and the work of the Holy Spirit. There is perhaps more ignorance concerning him than any other part of revealed truth. By many he is regarded as an undefinable influence. By many others he is supposed to come and go in a vague sort of way; now with the Christian and now absent from him; to-day with the church, to-morrow in some distant part of the world at work. All this is unscriptural, and must grieve him, who as certainly ABIDES with the true child of God as that Jesus died and arose again.

To know him aright has always meant POWER. To be ignorant of him has always meant confusion and ultimate defeat. The promise is, "Ye shall receive POWER, the Holy Ghost coming upon you." It is a possible thing for our creed to outrun our intelligence. We say again and again, "I believe in the Holy Ghost." Is it really true? With a single church believing in him we might move the world for God.

There is both ignorance and indifference concerning him, and the reason is most apparent. This is the "dispensation of the Spirit." It was ushered in at Pentecost. And Satan very well knows that so long as he can keep us in doubt as to the Spirit's work, or mystified as to his personality or presence, just so long he has nothing in us to fear. He cares not for your intellectual greatness—he can make a very snare of it—but he trembles when he sees one FILLED WITH THE HOLY GHOST.

Three propositions I would be glad to impress upon the mind, and in the light of them we shall study together the third person of the TRINITY: *First*, he has a personality. I might present many arguments to prove my statement. What stronger could there be than the words

RECEIVED YE THE HOLY GHOST?

of our Lord himself?—"And I will pray the Father, and he shall give you another Comforter, that he may abide with you forever; even the Spirit of truth; whom the world cannot receive, because it seeth him not, neither knoweth him: but ye know him; for he dwelleth with you, and shall be in you." (John xiv. 16, 17.) Notice the word "another." This indicates that he is to take the place of Jesus himself. Could anything less than a person take the place of a person? Notice also the personal pronouns repeated as the Master speaks of the Comforter. Refer also to John xvi. 13, 14, where the pronouns are again repeated, and then read what Paul writes to the Ephesians: "Grieve not the Holy Spirit of God." (Eph. iv. 30.) You surely cannot grieve an influence, and this is all that some would have us believe him to be. Either they are mistaken or the Apostle is in error. Which position do you take? *Second*, this is his dispensation. This being true we need not *wait* to be filled with all his fullness. Some have thought this necessary, and have quoted the experience of the waiting disciples at Pentecost as a proof; but it is to be remembered that they were waiting for the coming in of a dispensation, while we live in it. The Holy Ghost is in no place said to have left the world after Pentecost. *Third*, he will fill us when we have fulfilled the conditions. These will be explained later, but in a word they are as follows: First, make an unconditional surrender to him, and let him abide in you, not because it is his work to do so, but because you have bidden him. Throw open every door of your nature, and give him undisputed possession. Second, believe his promise: "That we might receive the *promise* of the Spirit through *faith*." (Gal. iii. 14.) Do these things, then trust him to do his work. He is no respecter of persons. I had in a former parish a young Irishman; all would declare him to be ignorant, and he was; but God marvelously used him. This was the secret. With a heart burdened for the men of the city, I called together a few of the men of the church, and laying before them the plan I had in mind, told them first of all that we could do nothing without the "infilling of the Holy Ghost." When this had been explained I noticed this man leave the room. He did not return while the meeting was in session. When I sought him I found him in one of the lower rooms of the church, literally on his face before God. He was in prayer. I shall never forget his petition: "O God, I plead with thee for this blessing;" then, as if God were showing him what was in the way, he said: "My Father, I will give up every known sin, only I plead with thee for power;" and then, as if his individual sins were passing before him, he said again and again: "I will give them up; I will give them up." Then, without any emotion, he rose from his knees, turned his face heavenward, and simply said: "And now I claim the blessing." For the first time he became sensible of my presence, and with a shining countenance he reached out his hands to clasp mine.

You could feel the very presence of the Spirit as he said: "I have received him; I have received him." And I believe he had, for in the next few months he led more than sixty men into the kingdom of God. His whole life had been transformed. He is just now being set apart to preach the gospel. We may differ as to the terms we use, but of this one thing we are all persuaded: there is awaiting many of us an enlarging vision of the Holy Ghost; for many could say, as did the disciples at Ephesus, "We have not so much as heard whether there be any Holy Ghost." (Acts xix. 2.) Whether we speak of this vision as a baptism, an infilling, or an anointing, may he show us himself, for we seek him and not a mere experience; the latter may be a thing of the moment, the former abides forever. (John xiv. 16.)

The forty-seventh chapter of Ezekiel gives to me a beautiful figure of what the Holy Spirit is, and the work he does. There is something in the source of the river, something in the direction in which it runs, something in its increasing depth as it nears the sea, and something in its fruited banks to lead us to him of whom we study. First have in mind the temple from which the river flows. It is suggestive. As you know, the temple in the Old Testament was divided into three main parts: first, the outer court, into which any child of Israel might make his way; second, the holy place, where only the white-robed priests might walk to and fro; and third, the holy of holies, where only the high priest might go, and that but once a year. This Old Testament temple typifies the temple of which Paul speaks in the New Testament: "Know ye not that ye are the temple of God, and that the Spirit of God dwelleth in you?" (1 Cor. iii. 16.) So the New Testament temple is yourself: "Which temple ye are." (1 Cor. iii. 17.) There is likewise a threefold division here. There is first the outer court, which corresponds to the body; the second court is the soul, the third court is the spirit. There are some people who never live beyond the outer court; but such do not understand what it is to live. It is a possible thing for the body to be controlled, or, at least, influenced by the Spirit, for we read: "He that raised up Christ from the dead shall also quicken your mortal bodies by his Spirit that dwelleth in you." (Rom. viii. 11.) It is apparent to all that he works in the soul, that is, the real self, the "ego." Here also the Spirit manifests himself, for we read: "Seeing ye have purified your souls in obeying the truth through the Spirit." (1 Peter i. 22.) But all must be aware that there are experiences deeper than the soul, and thus we are led to the spirit; this is the "holy of holies." It has been called "the secret place of the Most High." It is the place where God dwells. And here the Spirit works, for we read: "For ye are bought with a price: therefore glorify God in your body, and in your spirit, which are God's." (1 Cor. vi. 20.) And again: "The Spirit himself beareth witness with our spirit, that we are the children of God." (Rom. viii. 16.) And just as in the chapter to which reference has been made the sanctuary was so filled with the water that it rushed out by the way of the altar eastward, so we may be "filled with the Spirit," and so filled that there shall not only be communion, that is, for ourselves, but there may be the manifestation of power to others, illustrated in the flowing river. Our whole nature, body, soul, and spirit, may be swayed by his presence. If the temple pictures the real self, the man of to-day, then the water must stand for something. In the light of the Word of God, what would you say? I am sure we are making no mistake when we say that the water typifies the Holy Ghost. We surely have the right to say as much, for Jesus himself said it. Speaking to the woman of Samaria he said: "But whosoever drinketh of the water that I shall give him shall never thirst; but the water that I shall give him shall be in him a well of water springing up into everlasting life." (John iv. 14.) This is the "indwelling Spirit." But at the last day of the feast he made it still plainer when he said: "He that believeth on me, as the Scripture hath said, out of his belly shall flow rivers of living water. (But this spake he of the Spirit, which they that believe on him should receive: for the Holy Ghost was not yet given; because that Jesus was not yet glorified." (John vii. 38, 39.) This is the river flowing out from the sanctuary, running through the desert, healing the waters of the sea of life.

God often speaks to us by means of figures or types. This is an illustration. It may be both interesting and profitable to present other emblems of the Spirit, for each will come to us with a particular lesson.

I. THE WIND.

Sometimes he is spoken of under the figure of the wind, and this is generally when we would present his quickening, powerful, penetrating influence. There are many things about it which may be mentioned, all of which help us to understand the work of the Spirit the better. *First, the wind is invisible:* "The wind bloweth where it listeth, and thou hearest the sound thereof, but thou canst not tell whence it cometh, and whither it goeth: so is every one that is born of the

Spirit." (John iii. 8.) To my mind this beautifully presents to us one of the chief traits of the Spirit. He came not to draw attention to himself, but to the Son. We are told in another place concerning the Son, that he "made himself of no reputation, and took upon himself the form of a servant, and was made in the likeness of men." (Phil. ii. 7.) But herein was the love of the Spirit made manifest, for he came into the world without even the form of a servant. Suppose he had become incarnate, would there not have been a temptation to forget the incarnate Son in the contemplation of the incarnate Spirit? The Holy Ghost always magnifies the Lord Jesus Christ, *just as the river from the sanctuary ran eastward. Second, the wind is penetrating.* It is said that "nature abhors a vacuum." This is true, but it is likewise true that the Spirit abhors a vacuum, and we may rest assured that just as soon as the room is made for him he will fill us to overflowing. He abides with us now, but we may never feel the blessedness of his presence till we have forsaken all sin, surrendered all selfishness; for selfishness, sin, and worldliness cannot possess the child of God, if we would have the Spirit in his fullness. *Third, the wind is powerful.* A perfect illustration is found in the valley of dry bones. The valley was filled with the bones of the dead when the word of the Lord came to his servant to prophesy. John McNeil says he can imagine that Ezekiel looked down and he was afraid to say "Yes"; he looked up and he was afraid to say "No"; and so he answered, "O Lord God, thou knowest." "So I prophesied as I was commanded: and as I prophesied, there was a noise, and behold a shaking, and the bones came together, bone to bone. And when I beheld, lo, the sinews and the flesh came up upon them, and the skin covered them above: but there was no breath in them. Then he said unto me, Prophesy unto the wind, prophesy, son of man, and say to the wind, Thus saith the Lord God; Come from the four winds, O breath, and breathe upon these slain, that they may live. So I prophesied as he commanded me, and the breath came into them, and they lived, and stood up upon their feet, an exceeding great army." (Ezek. xxxvii. 7–10.) Surely this is a picture of all that the church might be, if we were, as individuals, "filled with the Spirit."

II. THE DOVE.

The dove is an emblem of the Holy Spirit, telling of his loving, tender, comforting work. This, of all the family of birds, is the most lovely. Its affection for its mate is almost pathetic. In its choice of a home, in the company it keeps, in its food, as well as in its very self, it is a beautiful picture of much that the Spirit may be in us. It is very helpful to me to know that when we receive him fully we become partakers of his nature. One could not be petulant, impatient, censorious, disagreeable, and be filled with his fullness. For when of his fullness we have received, we have "grace for grace," and what can this mean but a duplication of graces? (John i. 16.) In Paul's letter to the Galatians we read: "But the *fruit* of the Spirit is love, joy, peace, long-suffering, gentleness, goodness, faith, meekness, temperance: against such there is no law." (Gal. v. 22, 23.) You will notice that the word "fruit" is used in the singular number, and the inference must be that when we give ourselves up to the Spirit we have, not one of these graces, but all of them. First, the dove is a *patient* bird. Surely here it brings us a lesson of the Spirit. We have grieved him a thousand times, and yet he is the same tender, patient Spirit. As another has said: "Look at the way he is grieved." "Let no corrupt communication proceed out of your mouth, but that which is good to the use of edifying, that it may minister grace to the hearers. And grieve not the Holy Spirit of God, whereby ye are sealed unto the day of redemption. Let all bitterness, and wrath, and anger, and clamor, and evil speaking, be put away from you, with all malice: and be ye kind one to another, tender-hearted, forgiving one another, even as God for Christ's sake hath forgiven you." (Eph. iv. 29-32.) Compare this with the malice and evil speaking and censoriousness and slander that are notoriously common among professing Christians: we no longer wonder that the Holy Spirit is grieved. Every idle word, every unkind expression, every unholy thought grieves him, yet he tarries, waiting, yearning to fill us with his blessed presence and power. Second, the dove is a *loving* bird. We are well acquainted with the thought that God the Father loves us, and all must be sensible of the love of the Son, but of the love of the Spirit we are not so well informed. Yet Paul writes: "Now I beseech you, brethren, for the Lord Jesus Christ's sake, and for the love of the Spirit, that ye strive together with me in your prayers to God for me." (Rom. xv. 30.) "The love of the Spirit for every sinner who trusts in Christ for salvation can be measured only by the infinite and eternal love of the Father, and by the intense, self-sacrificing, boundless, and unchanging love of the Son." The first mention of the Spirit in the Old Testament suggests his love. We read: "And the Spirit moved upon the face of the waters." (Gen. i. 2.) The word "moved" in the Hebrew is literally "brooded," giving us the figure of the mother-bird hovering over her young; and if the word is studied more closely, it means to be "tremulous with love." This is the first picture, and he is "the same yesterday, to-day, and forever." To be "filled with the Spirit" thus means to be filled with this spirit. What a transformation it would mean to the individual and to the church! It would mean the reclaiming of the lost. In Isaiah we read: "But thou hast in love to my soul delivered it from the pit of corruption" (Isa. xxxviii. 17), and in the margin you read that it means "thou hast loved up my soul from the pit." It would mean the winning of souls.

HOW MAY I KNOW HIM?

It may be interesting to know that one of the first Salvation Army converts was thus won in France. Miss Booth had been singing and speaking for weeks. The people crowded around her only for the purpose of ridicule. At last, one evening when she had told her story with all the pathos with which she was capable, she went down from the platform and pushed her way through the crowd till she reached a fallen girl sitting in the rear of the room. She threw her arms about her neck and kissed her first upon one cheek, then upon the other, and she said as she did so, "My dear sister, I would that I could love you into the kingdom." The girl looked up in a startled way; pure lips like those had not touched her cheeks in many a day. She burst into tears. Miss Booth led her sobbing to the penitent form, where with true repentance she cried out for forgiveness. God saved her and she has been a good soldier ever since. Oh, that the church might be filled with this spirit!

> "Come, Holy Spirit, heavenly Dove,
> With all thy quickening powers:
> Come, shed abroad a Saviour's love,
> And that shall kindle ours."

III. THE OIL.

When God would reveal to us the healing, comforting, illuminating, and consecrating influences of the Spirit, he directs our minds to the oil, which shadows forth these characteristics. In a part of the description of the ancient tabernacle you read this sentence: "Oil for the light." (Ex. xxxv. 8.) This suggests the illustration another has used, letting the oil represent the Spirit, the wick the Christian, and the light stand for the result of the union of the two. There may be an abundance of oil and a plentiful supply of wick—there cannot be light until the two are brought together. I know the Spirit abides in us, and will forever, but there can never be a manifestation of his power till by the consent of our wills he has undisputed possession. The two may be brought together, and for a time the light is brilliant, but in a little while it is dim and flickering, and every housekeeper can understand the difficulty—the wick has become incrusted and must be trimmed. It is not enough for us to be right with God to-day, that we may have a manifestation of his power—we must KEEP RIGHT. The secret may be found in one sentence: "Confess your sins instantly." Even if the oil and the wick be brought together, there may be still little or no light, and the difficulty is, that there is a knot in the wick. It is not enough that the Spirit abide with us—this he does. The heart must be right in the sight of God. This was the difficulty with Simon the sorcerer. (Acts viii. 9–13.) When he tried to purchase with money the power of the Holy Ghost, he failed, because his heart was not right. We have, however, the privilege of believing that when the heart is right we have the very fullness of God himself. He is sometimes said to be the "oil to make the face shine." (Ps. civ. 15.) It is not possible to be filled with the Holy Ghost and then simply delight in the fact ourselves. God never bestows such a gift that we may consume it upon our own lusts. He is the outflowing river, and also reveals himself in the shining countenance. He is called the "oil of gladness." "Therefore God, thy God, hath anointed thee with the oil of gladness above thy fellows." (Ps. xlv. 7.) It is a most comforting thought that Satan cannot rob us of our life, for that is "hid with Christ in God." But he may deprive us of our JOY. It has been said that it is the work of Christ to bring us to heaven, but it is the work of the Spirit to bring heaven to us now. The Psalmist tells us: "In thy presence is fullness of joy" (Ps. xvi. 11); and since it is the work of the Spirit to lead us into God's presence, that means just one thing, namely, HEAVEN.

IV. THE WATER.

Water is typical of many things in the Bible. Sometimes it stands for judgment, sometimes for the Bible itself; but most frequently for the Holy Ghost does it stand as a type. Very many things may be said of the water, and the same things apply to the Holy Spirit.

First, the water is *free*. We may have it without money and without price. There is no truer thought than this about the Spirit. To rich or poor, to wise or ignorant, he will come with all his fullness. "By grace are we saved," and "by grace are we filled with his blessed presence." Second, the water is *refreshing*. "He leadeth me beside the still waters." (Ps. xxiii. 2.) When the journey is long, and the way dusty and hard to travel, and we are worn and weary, what is more refreshing than the springs of water? We stoop to drink and push out on our way rejoicing. All that the water is to the traveler, yea, a thousand times more, the Spirit of God is to the weary ones. The water in us is a well "springing up." It comes from the throne, it rises again to its source, for water always seeks its own level; and here is the thought of communion that is always refreshing. The water flowing out from us is a river, and that does not flow for itself, but for others. Thus the Spirit always leads us. And who has not found that in living for others he has made his own way brighter and his own path easier to travel? What is this but the very best of refreshment? Third, the water is *cleansing.* I am well aware that it is the work of the blood of Jesus Christ to "cleanse from all sin," but it is the work of the Spirit to bring that work to remembrance, so we may speak of him as cleansing. The word "cleansing" has several different meanings in the Word of God. Sometimes it is *katharos*, which means to "clear up." This must have been in Paul's mind when he said: "Be careful for nothing; but in everything by prayer and supplication with thanksgiving let your requests be made known unto God. And the peace of God, which passeth all understanding, shall keep your hearts and minds through Christ Jesus." (Phil. iv. 6, 7.) Careful for nothing, prayerful for everything, thankful for anything, as another has said. Sometimes it is *katharizo*, which means to "make clean"; and I am glad to know that this the Spirit of God surely does. We are told to keep ourselves "unspotted from the world." That would be most difficult were it not for the presence of the Spirit: with him it is easy. While in the mountains of Colorado, I noticed the miners going into the mine at the beginning of their "shifts"—their hands and faces were clean as they could make them; but at the end of the "shifts" it would be difficult to tell whether they were by nature black or white, and yet there was one part of the face which was just as clean as when they entered the mine: that was the ball of the eye; and that not because no impurities had touched it, for the mine was filled with such, but because there is a little tear-gland which keeps working all the time, and when the least speck touches the eye it washes it away. We are in the midst of sin and uncleanness in this world, but we may be kept clean every whit if we be only " filled with the Spirit." Keep in mind this river from the sanctuary, its source, its marvelous influence for good as it flows, and, not the least of all, keep in mind the direction in which it flowed. It will bear us on in our study till we are in the very " secret of his presence."

RECEIVED
YE THE
HOLY GHOST?

HOW MAY
I RECEIVE HIM?

Cap III   *HOW MAY I RECEIVE HIM?*

"That we might receive the promise of the Spirit through faith."—Gal. iii. 14.

THE Apostle Paul in his journeyings had come to Ephesus and found there a company of twelve men who were trying in a rude way to lead a holy life. They were John's disciples. They had been instructed by him in the doctrine of repentance, and it is supposed that they were members of the church of Corinth. Possibly because there was evidently something lacking in their testimony, or, as others have supposed, because they may have been denying the power of God in their lives or conversation, the Apostle puts to them the question, "Did ye receive the Holy Ghost when ye believed? And they said unto him, Nay, we did not so much as hear whether the Holy Ghost was." (Acts xix. 2, R. V.) It is not for a moment to be supposed that they were ignorant of the existence of the Spirit, for they were Jews, and their Scriptures teemed with references to his work. Then, too, they must have heard John speak of him. What they meant, undoubtedly, was that they had not heard of him as the abiding Comforter; and in this they were like many of the church-members of to-day. When Jesus ascended the Spirit came. It was his work, as it is now, to take up his abode in the hearts of believers. David might pray, "Take not thy Holy Spirit from me" (Ps. li. 11), but it would be a betrayal of ignorance for the child of God to offer such a petition to-day. There is not a thought in the New Testament suggesting that we "may grieve him away." What a difference there is between the Old Testament picture of the Spirit and the New Testament view of him! There he is represented as having his part in the work of creation: "And the Spirit of God moved upon the face of the waters." (Gen. i. 2.) He is there made known as the source of deliverance for his people: "And the Spirit of the Lord came upon him, and he judged Israel, and went out to war." (Judges iii. 10.) He was then, as now, the spring of all strength and courage: "And the Spirit of the Lord came mightily upon him, and he rent him as he would have rent a kid." (Judges xiv. 6.) But in the New Testament he is called the "Comforter": "And I will pray the Father, and he shall give you another Comforter." (John xiv. 16.) He is called the Teacher or Guide: "When the Spirit of truth is come, he will guide you into all truth." (John xvi. 13.)

There is an illustration of this truth in the Old Testament, which another has used. In the days of the flood, when Noah opened the window of the ark, the little dove flew over the waters, and finding no place to rest the sole of its foot, it came back again to the outstretched hand. He let it go

HOW MAY I RECEIVE HIM?

forth a second time. Flying hither and thither, it came back with an olive leaf in its mouth. He let it go yet the third time, and it found a resting-place for the sole of its foot, and it returned no more forever. The dove generally typifies the Spirit. In this case it at least tells a story of his coming. He came in the Old Testament, breathing upon Moses, burning in Isaiah, speaking through the lips of Abraham, but in the old dispensation he is not said to abide. He came when Jesus was crucified, and plucked, as it were, the olive leaf of peace from the cross (for the olive is the symbol of peace), and bore it back to the presence of God, saying, "Peace hath been made in the death of the Son." But he came the third time at Pentecost, with a rushing sound as of a mighty wind, and from that day to this he has never gone back. He has found his abiding-place in the hearts of believers.

It is interesting to notice how he is manifested, and how his coming is described. Sometimes he is represented as "clothing" his chosen ones, as, for example: "Tarry ye in the city of Jerusalem, until ye be endued with power from on high." (Luke xxiv. 49.) The word translated "endued" is elsewhere rendered "clothed." He is also represented as "poured out," to indicate his freeness: "Behold, I will pour out my spirit unto you." (Prov. i. 23.) He is represented as "filling," or taking complete possession of. It was predicted of John the Baptist, "He shall be filled with the Holy Ghost."

HOW MAY I RECEIVE HIM?

And to be "filled with the Spirit" is far more a scriptural expression than to be "baptized with the Holy Ghost." John the Baptist, Elizabeth, Zacharias, Jesus, Stephen, Barnabas, and Paul were all "filled with the Spirit," and we are told to be "filled with the Spirit." (Eph. v. 18.) There is a distinction here well worth our consideration. To be "baptized with the Spirit" may mean a pentecostal experience, a great rush of feeling, a change as great in the believer as the change from night to day. Not many people have such an experience, and for that reason multitudes are deprived of the real blessing of the Spirit's presence. To be "filled with the Spirit" may be almost the opposite of such an experience as that referred to. Mr. Meyer says that you can fill a cistern with water just as surely by letting little drops of water fall into it as by pouring in great hogsheads of water.

There are really two parts to the receiving of the Holy Ghost. First of all there is the baptism of the Spirit, as found in 1 Corinthians xii. 12, 13: "For as the body is one, and hath many members, and all the members of that body, being many, are one body: so also is Christ. For by one Spirit are we all *baptized* into one body, whether we be Jews or Gentiles, whether we be bond or free; and have been all made to drink into one Spirit." The second part is described in Acts i. 8: "But ye shall receive power, after that the Holy Ghost is come upon you: and ye shall be witnesses unto me both in Jerusalem, and in all Judea, and in Samaria, and

HOW MAY I RECEIVE HIM?

unto the uttermost part of the earth." This is power, and depends upon one's moral condition. According to this outline, then, every child of God has received the baptism of the Spirit; he is also, because of this, a member of the body of Christ. This experience can never be repeated; so, then, it is unscriptural for the Christian to be talking about the baptism of the Holy Ghost when he has already received it: but he may be filled with the Spirit and then, because of his moral condition, lose the power of the Spirit, as we find the disciples doing. They were filled in the first chapter of Acts, and in the fourth chapter of Acts, thirty-first verse, it is said again that "they were all filled with the Holy Ghost, and they spake the word of God with boldness." If you will study the second and third chapters, you will find that the disciples had lack of courage, and for that very reason had lost their blessing; but when the Spirit came upon them again, they became possessed of the very thing in which they had been lacking. There is, therefore, one baptism, many fillings. The Holy Ghost as certainly abides in us as that Jesus Christ stands to-day at the right hand of the Father. We need only to remove the hindrances in order that he may manifest his power; so, therefore, "Take ye away the stone." I am persuaded that to be "filled with the Spirit" we must make a complete and definite surrender and then trust him to do his work. He will, doubtless, begin in some little way to manifest his presence, just as it were drop by drop. To-day a new pathos in the voice, to-morrow a new touch of the hand, and so on day by day, till his presence in all its fullness will be a blessed reality. The first step, however, in this blessing, as the first step into the "life of the eternal," is a step of faith. I used to be greatly troubled by the recitation of personal experiences in many of the public meetings. One would say, "I was converted such a year;" another, such a month; another, such a day or hour; and to me it was discouraging, for I could not tell the year, much less the day. But I am distressed about it no longer, and for two reasons: First, I should know I was living physically even if I did not know my birthday, and I may know that I am living spiritually even though I do not know when I "passed from death into life." My second reason is found in the fact that I have a better experience: I have had my eyes opened to the truth of the Spirit; and if you will allow me to choose between the man who has had a definite experience in conversion, and knows little of the Holy Ghost, and the man who may be uncertain as to the time of his conversion, but knows about the third person of the Trinity, I will choose the latter every time, for I am certain that I may be a Christian and not know when I crossed the line, but I cannot be a Christian with an experience of power until I know something definite about the Holy Ghost.

What vague ideas and views we have concerning him! We think of him as coming and going, with us to-day, away

HOW MAY I RECEIVE HIM?

from us to-morrow. We pray for his outpouring. We cry out in sermon, in song, and in prayer, "Come, Holy Ghost," as if he were still in the skies, when the fact is that he abides with us ALWAYS and is nearer to us than our right hand. He may not always be manifesting his power, but that is because we have placed some hindrance in the way. In a sense, there is a twofold bestowal of the Spirit, but it is like this, quoting from Dr. James H. Brooks in his work on the Holy Spirit: "We are told that on the evening of the same day that our Lord arose from the grave, 'when the doors were shut where the disciples were assembled for fear of the Jews, came Jesus and stood in the midst, and saith unto them, Peace be unto you. And when he had so said, he showed unto them his hands and his side. Then were the disciples glad, when they saw the Lord. Then said Jesus to them again, Peace be unto you: as my Father hath sent me, even so send I you. And when he had said this, he breathed on them, and saith unto them, Receive ye the Holy Ghost.' (John xx. 19–22.) No one can imagine that these solemn words were uttered in vain, or that the disciples did not then receive the Holy Ghost. It makes the language and action of our risen Lord all the more significant when we remember that this is the only place in the New Testament where the word rendered 'breathed' is found, and that the Saviour never elsewhere is said to breathe on any one." The other was the bestowal of the Spirit at Pentecost, when they were qualified

HOW MAY I RECEIVE HIM?

as witnesses. Hence there is a twofold bestowal of the Spirit: one secret and inward, within closed doors as it were; the other open and outward in its manifestations. The former is never repeated; the latter is repeated over and over according to the measure of our faith and of our desire. The former was Christ's gift to his servants; it was a special blessing for a special purpose. The latter was in fulfilment of the promise, "Ye shall receive power, after that the Holy Ghost is come upon you: and ye shall be witnesses unto me." (Acts i. 8.)

One word needs to be sounded over and over again if we are to be the recipients of this blessing. That word is "surrender." The very moment we have fulfilled this condition then rest assured that he will begin the manifestation of himself. We are not to suppose that we may mark out the channel in which he is to run, for the WILL must be given up in this as in other things. It is generally supposed, however, that to be filled with the Spirit always means power from the human standpoint, and this is anything but true. It always means power; but power in the estimation of God may mean defeat in the thought of men. It is to be remembered that Peter was " filled with the Holy Ghost," and preached the sermon at Pentecost, while Stephen was " filled with the Holy Ghost," and was stoned to death: one was as great a victory in the sight of God as the other.

Not infrequently the children of God go mourning after this blessing and find

HOW MAY I RECEIVE HIM?

it not, and for the reason that they are seeking the consciousness of the blessing rather than the Spirit himself. We have nothing to do with the consciousness: we are to have faith in God, believing in the indwelling Spirit when with great emotion and much enthusiasm we are working, as well as when without either we do his bidding. Consciousness of power may be a very dangerous thing. There is hardly an old horse with which we are familiar which we would be willing to drive if that horse were conscious of his power. He could break away from us in an instant—but he is not conscious. We have the consciousness, and he has the power, and so we guide him whithersoever we will. Let us just believe God, and let him be conscious of all that we may accomplish. It is ours just to be submissive.

I. HOW MAY I RECEIVE HIM?

First. One of the most important steps with which I am familiar is this: do not seek to know him, first of all, that you might teach or preach with power. This is not the way to the blessing. Again, do not seek to know him that you may have the peace of which others have spoken who have known him in all his fullness. This is not the first step. But rather, bid him abide in you, that, first of all, HE MAY HAVE POWER OVER YOURSELF. He is the fire, and will, if allowed, burn out the dross. He is the water, and he will keep the temple clean. Then only may we expect to be

HOW MAY I RECEIVE HIM?

used. Mr. Moody has so many times said: "God does not seek silver vessels, and he does not require gold ones for his service, but he must have clean ones."

Second. The second step has already been indicated. It is this: SURRENDER FULLY. To give up ninety-nine parts of the nature and withhold the hundredth is to put a hindrance in the way of the blessing. If a contagious disease had been raging in a certain house, and you had a desire to live in the house, you know that you would not do it until every room had been purified. If every room but one had been fumigated, and that the smallest room, you know that you would not occupy the house. Nor will the Holy Spirit work with power in the life till it has all been surrendered to him, till it has all been made clean by true confession: then make ready for the blessing which God has promised. I can remember when God opened my eyes to this truth. I had been struggling for five years, I had had visions of his power and glimpses of what I might be if I were "filled with the Spirit," but all this time, like the disciples at Ephesus, there was a great lacking. At last I reached the place where I felt that I was willing to make the surrender. I reached it by the path marked out by Mr. Meyer when he said: "If you are not ready to surrender everything to God, are you ready to say, 'I am willing to be made willing about everything'?" That seemed easy, and alone before God I simply said, "I am willing." Then he made the way easy. He brought before me my ambition, then my personal ease, then my home, then other things came to me, and I simply said, "I will give them up." And last of all my "will" was surrendered about everything. Then without any emotion, for, as Mr. Meyer said, it was "faith without emotion," I said, "My Father, I now claim from thee the infilling of the Holy Ghost." From that moment to this he has been a living reality. I never knew what it was to love my family before, I question if they ever knew what it was to love me, although we had called ourselves happy in the love of each other. I never knew what it was to study the Bible before, and why should I? For had I not just then found the key? I never knew what it was to preach before. "Old things are passed away;" in my Christian experience, "behold, all things are become new."

Third. The third step is found in Paul's letter to the Galatians, where he says: "That we might receive the promise of the Spirit through faith." (Gal. iii. 14.) You will notice that it does not say, "That we might receive the Spirit through faith." It is often so quoted. This would be unscriptural, for we have the Spirit. He is with us to abide forever. It is just to believe his word; and the third step is one of FAITH. We say to the man seeking Christ, and yet who hesitates because he is without feeling—we say to him, "It is faith first, then feeling after;" and so we say to all who seek the infilling of the Holy Ghost, "Receive the promise by faith."

HOW MAY I RECEIVE HIM?

These steps do not of necessity follow in logical order, for the last may be first if one so desires; but the next step suggested would be this: keep your eyes fixed upon Christ. There is an Old Testament illustration of this. When Elijah and Elisha were journeying toward the place of the translation, you will remember that the people came out at Bethel, Gilgal, and other places, and entreated Elisha to tarry with them for a season, and Elijah said, "Tarry, I pray thee, here." (2 Kings ii. 6.) "And he said, As the Lord liveth, and as thy soul liveth, I will not leave thee." (2 Kings ii. 6.) "And it came to pass, when they were gone over, that Elijah said unto Elisha, Ask what I shall do for thee, before I be taken away from thee.

RECEIVED YE THE HOLY GHOST?

And Elisha said, I pray thee, let a double portion of thy spirit be upon me. And he said, Thou hast asked a hard thing: nevertheless, if thou see me when I am taken from thee, it shall be so unto thee; but if not, it shall not be so." (2 Kings ii. 9, 10.) Suddenly, as they talked, the chariot of fire appeared, and Elijah became a passenger. I suppose Elisha was too greatly surprised to speak at first; then he cried out, "My father, my father, the chariot of Israel, and the horsemen thereof." (2 Kings ii. 12.) And Elijah dropped upon him, I imagine, the old mantle, for it is said that he took it up. Suppose he had wrapped it around him, saying, "How comfortable it is!" what benefit would it have been? But he did not do this. He had his reward when the old mantle fell upon him. He simply stood on the banks of the Jordan and used the mantle as his master had used it, and the waters parted as before. We are given the Spirit not that we may consume him upon our own lusts, but in order that we may be in this world as Jesus himself. Do you remember his words, "Verily, verily, I say unto you, He that believeth on me, the works that I do shall he do also; and greater works than these shall he do; because I go unto my Father"? (John xiv. 12.) What is this but Elijah and Elisha again? Here is the secret of it all: KEEP YOUR EYES FIXED ON A TAKEN-UP MASTER. Elisha had the spirit of his master before. I suppose he had followed him so closely that he had absorbed the very spirit of Elijah; but it was the double portion he was seeking, and that he received. So it is with us if we are in Christ: we have the indwelling Spirit; but we need, and we must have, the double portion, and this comes with a knowledge of the Spirit, which every one may have in Christ.

II. SUGGESTIONS.

It may be helpful to ask the question, "Why have I not received him?" This may be for many reasons.

First. It may be because we have disobeyed some clear command of the Master: if at any time in the past we have broken a thread in the weaving of a garment, we need not expect to know about the fullness of the Spirit until we have made the past right with God. If it was an unkind word spoken, an inconsistent

HOW MAY I RECEIVE HIM?

action which caused another to stumble or fall, if it is some unforgiven sin, then make it right; and then, too, it is not enough to get right, as we often hear, but we must keep right. And there is no way by which this may be so easily accomplished as just to be quick to obey God's least commands. Be very sensitive to his leadings and teachings; offer this prayer of David's: " Search me, O God, and know my heart: try me, and know my thoughts: and see if there be any wicked way in me, and lead me in the way everlasting." (Ps. cxxxix. 23, 24.)

Second. The second suggestion may be embraced with the first, but it is made distinct, at least for the sake of emphasis. It may be that the difficulty is found in the fact that you have not confessed your sin. In a western city a gentleman approached the evangelist laboring in the city with this question: "Can you tell me why it is that I have no power in my Christian life? I have a class of men in the Sunday-school, and have had for three years, and have never been able to lead one of them to Christ." The evangelist replied, "It may be because your heart is not right with God, and that you are hiding some sin." The man's face became pale, and then in the secrecy of the minister's room he made his confession: "Twelve years ago I was a clerk in a mercantile establishment in the city of P——. One night in balancing my books I had two hundred dollars for which I could not account; my books were balanced, but the money was there. The books balanced the next day and the next week, and the money was still not accounted for. Then the devil came to me to say, 'Use it; no one will ever know it, and you can put it back.' God pity me! I took it, and all these years I have had it. Here it is," he said, handing it to the evangelist. "I cannot take it," he said; "you will have to make restitution." The man sprang to his feet, exclaiming: "I can never do it. I have a position now worth twenty thousand dollars a year to me, and I should lose it if I were even suspected of being dishonest in the past." "It is either restitution or no power," said the evangelist. The man was still for a moment; then, rising to his feet, he exclaimed, "I will do it if I die." He made his way to the city where the wrong had been committed, into the private office of the man against whom he had sinned, and made confession. The Christian merchant listened to his words; then, rising, he closed the door of the office, and said, "Let us pray about it." They fell on their knees, and when the prayer was offered the merchant said to him: "Go back to your work, and God's blessing go with you. I forgive you just as freely as he does." The man came back to his home with his face shining. The next Sunday he sat down before his class to tell them of Christ. He said to them: "I never knew till this week why it was that I could not get you for Christ. I have now found out. It was because I was not right myself." Then, turning to his class, he made such a plea as he had never made before, and with the result that every member of his class accepted

Christ as Saviour, and a few Sundays after joined the church of which he was a member. It is very easy to understand why. He had simply gotten right with God, and then the Spirit, who had been abiding in him all the time, used him; and that is always the Spirit's way.

Third. Again, it may be that we have too little communion with God in his Word. Have you not always noticed that when one knew his Bible he knew the Spirit well? It is the poverty of the knowledge of the Word of God that makes us poor in our understanding of the Spirit. He inspired holy men of old to write the Book. Why should we not know him if we know his thought? When one of our Christian philanthropists was presiding, a number of years ago, at a great Peace Congress in

Washington, in the midst of their deliberations a company of Indians came in. They were asked to speak, and through an interpreter an old chief made the following remarks: "We have come here to see the Great Father, the President. We have come to ask him to help our people." And then looking about on the crowd assembled, he said: "Our people are not like yours, our women and children are not like yours, our homes are not like yours. Can you tell the Indian," he said, "what medicine he must take to make him right?" Then Major-General O. O. Howard, who was a member of the congress, the man who wears an empty coat-sleeve to the honor of his country, the man who is a loyal soldier of Christ as well, sprang to the speaker's desk, and with his one arm

HOW MAY I RECEIVE HIM?

raised aloft the Bible, exclaiming, while every one was thrilled: "Mr. Speaker, tell him this is the Good Medicine." And it is. It is the medicine to make right the world's wrongs; it is the medicine to purify the heart; and to know this is to know the Spirit, while to know the Spirit is POWER.

RECEIVED YE THE HOLY GHOST?

WHAT OF THE RESULT?

Cap IV

WHAT OF THE RESULT?

"But ye shall receive power, after that the Holy Ghost is come upon you: and ye shall be witnesses unto me both in Jerusalem, and in all Judea, and in Samaria, and unto the uttermost part of the earth."
—Acts i. 8.

REFERRING again to the river from the sanctuary, we get the best answer to this question. The river ran into the desert. The Spirit of God always leads us into the world, that we may go to the lost and tell them of life, bidding them in the name of Christ and on the authority of the Word and by the power of the Spirit to believe in him, that their position may be changed—a good illustration of which is Mephibosheth. He dwelt at Lo-debar (which means "the place of no pasture"), but through the kindness of David, for Jonathan's sake, he is brought to the king's table that he may have plenty. The river was healing, for we read that, running into the sea, the waters thereof were healed. The river was life-giving: "And it shall come to pass, that everything that liveth, which moveth, whithersoever the rivers shall come, shall live." (Ezek. xlvii. 9.) It is fruit-producing and food-providing. What a river it was! But there was one thing it could not do, namely, change the marshy places: "But the miry places thereof and the marshes thereof shall

WHAT OF THE RESULT?

not be healed; they shall be given to salt." (Ezek. xlvii. 11.) The Spirit does not come to improve man's carnal nature. "That which is born of the flesh is flesh," and always will be. But all that the river does, as described above, we may have repeated in our lives. Our position is "in the world, but not of it." We have had placed in our keeping for wounded hearts the very balm of Gilead. We have the words of eternal life, we have the very bread of heaven—in fact, we have all things in Christ. There would be a marvelous change in the church as well as in the individual if only we were "filled with the Spirit." We have to-day in the church men enough, and they have money enough, and, humanly speaking, we have power enough to put to flight the enemy, if only we were "filled with the Holy Ghost."

I have a friend in New York City, a most remarkable woman. She has turned away from her social position, given up, for the time being, her home, with the full consent of her family, and devotes all her time and her strength to the rescuing of "fallen girls." She has literally prayed up the Door of Hope, an institution which is a refuge for all such; and there is never a night so dark or so long but the doors of this home are open for the wanderer. One night at midnight, leaving her home, going out on an expedition through the slums of New York, she held in her hand a beautiful pink rose. She said to one of her friends, "I will give this rose to the vilest girl I meet in my wanderings."

WHAT OF THE RESULT?

She made her way to Mulberry Street, a place which is a veritable hell. It is the place where men and women go when all hope has fled from them and they are ready to throw themselves into perdition. In one of the subcellars, surrounded by some of New York's worst characters, was the girl whom Mrs. Whittemore, in her mind, had been seeking. This was the description she gave of her: her hair was torn out as if she had been in a recent brawl, as they found out afterward she had; her face bore the marks of sin; her clothing hung in rags from her poor, thin shoulders; her feet were pressing their way through her old shoes; her eyes were as blue as the sky, and for that reason she was called by her companions "Blue Bird." As my friend stood looking at her, she told me that the vilest profanity she had ever heard was falling from her lips. She pushed her way through the crowd of men, and placed in the girl's hand the pink rose, saying as she did so: "My dear, if ever in your life you want a friend, come to the Door of Hope, and I will be a mother to you." The girl at once replied, "I'm too sinful to be saved or helped." But Mrs. Whittemore left her that night with the prayer that she might come. Several days after, just as my friend was going into the Door of Hope, she found Blue Bird, looking more miserable than before. The first thought was one of discouragement, and the second almost a determination to put her out into the street, for it did seem impossible, even with God, to help her. Then she said:

WHAT OF THE RESULT?

"I looked down at her in her misery, and thought, There is a soul for whom Christ died, and if she had been the only lost one in the world he would have suffered and died for her. Then I forgot her sin and saw her soul. I forgot her misery, and my heart was filled with love for her. I stooped, and taking her sin-stained face in both my hands, I kissed her first upon one cheek, then upon the other, and that broke her heart; she fell sobbing before me. We put her in bed, nursed her back to a semblance of strength, and then she went forth, herself a missionary, down into the Mulberry Street dives, out into Sing Sing prison, everywhere where she felt that she might win a soul for Christ. She went by day and night. After a few months of active service God called her to himself, but she had been instrumental in leading over one hundred girls like herself into the knowledge of a Saviour." I asked my friend, Mr. Hadley, Jerry McAuley's successor in the old Water Street Mission: "Mr. Hadley, how did Blue Bird look: was she beautiful?" His reply was: "If you had seen her face in repose you might have said that she was homely, for her face still bore the marks of her sin; but," said he, "if you had seen her in the Water Street Mission, and heard her tell the story of her conversion, and then seen her stand with face uplifted, as if she were looking into the very face of Him who had made her free, and heard her as she repeated his name over and over—'JESUS! JESUS! JESUS!'—you would have said, I am sure, that she looked like an angel." Then I asked him, "What was the secret of her power?" He gave me two reasons. "First of all," he said, "she was fully saved; then after that" he said, "she was filled with the Spirit. Blue Bird had never a thought of her own; she belonged to him body, soul, and spirit." And when he told me that, I said: "Blessed God, if thou canst take a poor fallen girl and so fill her with thy Spirit that she could be transformed into a soul-winner, thou canst fill me;" and I believe he can—nay, more, I believe he did; and what he has done for one he can do for all, for, as has been said, he is no respecter of persons.

But there are certain particular results which would be manifest in the life of every one who would give the Spirit undisputed possession of his life.

First. We should know God better: "For what man knoweth the things of a man, save the spirit of man which is in him? even so the things of God knoweth no man, but the Spirit of God. Now we have received, not the spirit of the world, but the Spirit which is of God; that we might know the things that are freely given to us of God. Which things also we speak, not in the words which man's wisdom teacheth, but which the Holy Ghost teacheth; comparing spiritual things with spiritual. But the natural man receivth not the things of the Spirit of God: for they are foolishness unto him: neither can he know them, because they are spiritually discerned." (1 Cor. ii. 11–14.)

Second. We should be better able to apprehend Christ, for you will remember that the Spirit came into the world to testify of him. There is a hint of this in the very course of the river which ran from the sanctuary. There would have been no point at all if any other direction had been given as the course of the river, but the east is most significant. The camp of Israel was always pitched toward the east—the sun-rising—because Israel was looking and longing for the coming of the Messiah. The east is connected with the resurrection and with the coming glory of Christ. What can the course of the river signify but the fact that the Spirit always runs, if we may so speak of him, toward Christ? —to know one is to know the other. Do you not remember that when Jesus breathed on the disciples and said, "Receive ye the Holy Ghost," it was after

His resurrection? Was he not then, in the gift of the Spirit, just giving them the first taste of "resurrection life" for themselves? And this is, in fact, what the indwelling of the Spirit may mean for every one. We are "risen with Christ," and the Spirit just reveals to us what that means. And yet with all the joy that is imparted here in this present time, this is but the earnest of what is coming by and by. He is called the Earnest, as, for example: "Now he which stablisheth us with you in Christ, and hath anointed us, is God; who hath also sealed us, and given the earnest of the Spirit in our hearts." (2 Cor. i. 21, 22.) An earnest is often represented as a pledge, but this does not give the real idea. It is rather part of the purchase-money, paid down

WHAT OF THE RESULT?

as the guaranty and security that the full amount will be handed over at the time stipulated in the contract. The meaning, then, is simply this: all that the indwelling Spirit may have meant to you in the past in the way of sweetness of experience, depth of joy, delight in communion, or manifestation of power—these things are just the foretaste of what is coming after a while. When the fullness of time is come, if this is the first-fruit, then what must the harvest be? Here we have thought about him, he has come to us in the night visions, we have said over and over his dear name, but then we shall see him and we shall be like him.

"Well, the delightful day will come
When my dear Lord will bring me home,
And I shall see his face.

> Then with my Saviour, Brother, Friend,
> A blest eternity I'll spend,
>   Triumphant in his grace."

Third. There will be growth. This would naturally follow because of what we have found the Spirit to be. He is the wind, the dew, the rain, and many other things, all of which induce growth in the natural world. There will be a growth downward: "Rooted and built up in him" (Col. ii. 7); growth upward: "Into him in all things, which is the head, even Christ" (Eph. iv. 15); growth outward in all the fruit of the Spirit. I am sure that, with this thought of growth in mind, many of the troublesome questions in the life of the church might be settled. Paul had this in mind when he said, "When I was a child, I spake as a child, I understood as a child,

WHAT OF THE RESULT?

I thought as a child: but when I became a man, I put away childish things." (1 Cor. xiii. 11.)

Try the question of the so-called popular amusements of the day with this idea of growth in mind. See how quickly it could be settled. It is not to be denied that there is a certain kind of pleasure in some of the things which are manifestly inconsistent in the lives of professing Christians. But it is just as true that the real Christian has in his life that which is far beyond the mere pleasure of the world —that they are not comparable: but there must be growth to appreciate this. You remember the island of which we read in mythology—the island on which the sirens sang so sweetly that when a ship would come near its sailors would be charmed with the music. They would leave their posts of duty, and the vessel would be wrecked on the rocks. Then the sirens would put forth from the island to gather the spoil. One day a vessel neared the island having Ulysses as commander. He filled the sailors' ears with wax, and bade them fasten him to the mast, and then forbade their releasing him, whatever his commands might be under the spell of the music. When they neared the island it seemed as if the sirens had never sung so sweetly. Ulysses struggled to be free; he shouted to the sailors to let him go, but they did not hear him, and they would not let him go. They passed the island in safety. This was one way of going by. It is the way some would have us settle the question

WHAT OF THE RESULT?

of "amusements for the church." But there is a better way. Another vessel came near the island of the sirens. The officers did not order wax to be placed in the sailors' ears, neither was the commander fastened to the mast. The sirens sang their sweetest songs, they played their most entrancing music, but the sailors did not turn their heads to listen, and for this reason: they had Orpheus on board, and Orpheus sang a sweeter song than the sirens ever knew. Thanks be unto God, we may have Orpheus on board: we have a peace the world can never know! But the ear must be trained to hear the music. Just as when Jesus was on earth, at one time it was said: "Then came there a voice from heaven, saying, I have both glorified it, and will glorify it again. The people therefore that stood by, and heard it, said that it thundered: others said, An angel spake to him." (John xii. 28, 29.) I believe it was the voice of God to him—what some called thunder, and others an angel's voice. He called the voice of God to himself; they heard with their ears, he with his soul.

There is something very suggestive to me in the fact that the river increased in depth as it ran to the sea. "And when the man that had a line in his hand went forth eastward, he measured a thousand cubits." (Ezek. xlvii. 3.) At this first measurement the "waters were to the ankles." I use my ankles to walk with; I could hardly walk without them; and I believe it to be a hint, at least, of the fact that when one has been filled with the Holy Ghost he will manifest the fact in his daily walk. What is it to walk in the Spirit? It is to have him so enthroned in the soul, and to live in such habitual and uninterrupted communion with him, that we do not take a step without his direction. It is to recognize his abiding presence, to heed his slightest suggestion, to be lifted into a purer and sweeter atmosphere than that which surrounds the world. The second measurement, and the "waters were to the knees." I bow the knees to pray. No one really knows how to pray until he knows the Spirit. How often we wonder why our prayers have not been answered! I doubt not but that the real reason could be found just here: we did not ask in the right way. "Likewise the Spirit also helpeth our infirmities: for we know not what we should pray for as we ought: but the Spirit himself maketh intercession for us with groanings which cannot be uttered." (Rom. viii. 26.) The third measurement, and the "waters were to the loins." The loins are always in the Scripture the symbol of strength, and what can this suggest but that the Spirit is the strength of our life? With him temptation is easily met, burden-bearing becomes a delight, and we can do all things just because he fills us. "Afterward he measured a thousand; and it was a river that I could not pass over: for the waters were risen, waters to swim in, a river that could not be passed over." (Ezek. xlvii. 5.) There is one thing about swimming which every swimmer knows, namely, this: when he swims he brings into play

WHAT OF THE RESULT?

every muscle of his body—not one is inactive. Thanks be unto God, the Spirit may sway every power of my being: the heart purified, the mind quickened, the soul uplifted! He gives me a new name, a new song, a new hope—in fact, "old things are passed away;" the very world itself becomes new.

But one of the very best things we read about the river is this: "And by the river upon the bank thereof, on this side and on that side, shall grow all trees for meat, whose leaf shall not fade, neither shall the fruit thereof be consumed: it shall bring forth new fruit according to his months, because their waters they issued out of the sanctuary: and the fruit thereof shall be for meat, and the leaf thereof for medicine." (Ezek. xlvii. 12.) There was new fruit every month—what a river it must have been! I do not know anything better about the Spirit than this: he brings not only things old, but things new, before us. We shall not need to live on old manna if we have him. We shall not need to be rehearsing old experiences told a thousand times if we know him; but the world will be a new world, the Bible a new book, all things will wear a different face to us, if we be "filled with the Spirit." I know of no better illustration to make plain what his indwelling may mean than that which has been given us in the life and death of one of earth's noble women. Over in London, some time ago, a noble woman died. God touched her eyes, and they were closed; her heart, and it ceased its beating. They carried her into one of

WHAT OF THE RESULT?

the greatest auditoriums, that the city and the world might pay her honor. A representative of the Queen honored herself by being present. Lords and ladies were there; the rich people of England came to look and weep. At last the poor people came pressing their way into the great building. The weeping thousands passed beside the sleeping woman. At last a very poor woman made her way down the aisle. She had every mark of poverty; she carried a child on one arm, and led another by the hand. When she reached the coffin she put the baby on the floor, loosed the clasp of the older child's hand, and then stooped to kiss the glass which covered the face. She thereby stopped the passing of the throng. The guard, stepping forward, took her by the shoulder, saying as he did so: "Woman, you will have to move on; you are stopping the people." She lifted her face to his for a moment, and then, turning to the surging mass of people in the building, she cried out: "My friends, I will not move on! I have walked sixty miles, and carried my baby, that I might look upon this woman's face. She saved my boys from hell, and I have a right to look and to weep." Then bending down she kissed again and again the glass covering the face, while the multitude sobbed in sympathy with her. Who was she sleeping in the coffin yonder? Why, that was Mrs. Booth, the mother of the Salvation Army, one of the grandest women God has ever called into his service, and I am sure you know why: not because her social position was better

WHAT OF THE RESULT?

than yours, for that might not be true; not because her intellectual qualifications were superior to yours, for that might be untrue; but because she was filled with the Holy Ghost. That is always the secret of POWER.

www.ingramcontent.com/pod-product-compliance
Lightning Source LLC
Chambersburg PA
CBHW020118170426
43199CB00009B/562